WHAT WOULD YOU DO?

WHAT WOULD YOU DO?

☞ MEL PORETZ ☜

FAWCETT COLUMBINE / NEW YORK

A Fawcett Columbine Book
Published by Ballantine Books

Library of Congress Catalog Card Number: 93-90940

ISBN: 0-449-90762-7

Cover design by Kathleen Lynch
Text design by Beth Tondreau Design/Mary A. Wirth

Manufactured in the United States of America

First Edition: August 1994

10 9 8 7 6 5 4 3 2 1

To Dr. James G. Murray
University Professor, Adelphi University, Garden City, New York

I'd give anything to have had him as my *first* English Lit. professor when I started college at seventeen instead of having had him as my first postgrad English Lit. professor when I was fifty-eight. I'd have known him, been devoted to him, and been enriched by him all that much longer. But thank the good Lord I *did* have him!

Acknowledgments

Special and grateful thanks to the computer maven who took my ouija board and abacus and burned them, replacing them with the most intelligent rendition of this book's complex database that I could hope for. My genius friend's name is Jim Hallahan, and his company is Computer Assistance Company of Lake Success, New York.

And while I'm in so thankful a mood, my life, and all it has been since the age of twenty-three, I owe to my wife, Inez Poretz.

Introduction

This is a book about choices, both the non-gut-wrenching kind we make every day of our lives and the emotionally charged nerve-rackers that take their toll in the making and, all too often, in the aftermath.

It's a book about how a wide swath of Americans, selected in a scientifically drawn process according to census statistics dealing with gender, age, income, and education, responded to a barrage of dilemmas they were confronted with in a totally confidential mail survey.

Sixteen thousand questionnaires were mailed out, and I received 2,810 responses, thereby getting a 17.6 percent return rate that is exceptional in the world of mail-in surveys and which makes the survey statistically reliable to plus-or-minus 3.5 to 4 percent. The respondents live in all fifty states and include every layer of American social and economic circumstance, from the wealthy to the barely surviving, and from those who simply checked off the answers and let it go at that to the verbose, who went to great lengths to tell me what was on their minds. For example, I received this reply (rather than the asked-for YES/NO answer) in response to the question "If you found a major credit card, would you keep it and use it, or return it?" (see page 23) The answer given was "I stop my car to help the blind cross an intersection. I've chased robbers till cops can be reached; interfered in child abuse cases and animal abuse. Found wallet with money and returned wallet empty of \$\$ but with all credit cards. Does that give you the answer you're looking for?"

Another dilemma! Is this a YES or a NO?

Where did the ponderous, brow-wrinkling questions in the survey come from? From tracts on philosophy, from everyday experiences of family and friends, and from dilemmas of growing up (such as, could Superman beat up Batman?). I didn't bother with medieval theologians who debated about the number of angels that could dance on the head of a pin, but I did tap Kierkegaard and Twain, Will Rogers and Woody Allen, and especially the hallowed pages of the *New York Times*, whose headlines often trumpet news of moral dilemmas of the most convoluted sort (the most interesting of which occupy sixteen pages of this book).

Other questions arose from firsthand personal experience, like the time the author was sitting at a reading table in the second-floor Reference Department of the New York Public Library. Out of the nearby women's rest room came a young woman wearing a neatly tailored two-piece suit and medium heels and carrying a zipper case under her arm.

The dilemma: to act? to tell? to do nothing?! For trailing to the ground from under her jacket was a strip of toilet tissue, easily the length of a full-grown alligator. A second white streamer led out from where it had adhered to the heel of her right shoe.

His choice made, our hero inserted a page marker in his book and, rising from his chair, waited for the woman to pass his table so that the end of the tissue trailing from her waist was right in front of him. When she did so, he stuck out his foot, pinning the errant strip. But this succeeded in liberating only that portion of the tissue that touched the floor. A length of toilet paper running from her waist to midcalf was still tucked into her skirt, too high up to get rid of it by stepping on it. It would have to be removed with a yank.

Our hero, with one hop, one skip, and an agile grande jeté, managed to ensure that the particle dragging from her shoe curled lifelessly on the floor. As for the last remaining piece, there was only one more chance to grab for it before the Charmin lady would be out of the building. So he followed her to the exit of the building, where he declared, "Permit me to get the door." Thus positioned on her left as she went through, he released the door prematurely so that it slammed into her left hip, momentarily distracting her and providing him with a split second to take this one and only remaining swipe at the toilet paper tail. Excalibur! He had the trophy!

(How would others respond to this poser? See for yourself, on page 140.)

The *New York Times* could be counted on to be a wellspring of dilemmas, most of them, regrettably, all too vivid. Stories about John Gotti's highly publicized trial in the summer of '92 resounded with reports of jury irregularities, which were highlighted by one juror's request to be excused from the balance of the proceedings on the grounds that she would feel too frightened if she had to render a guilty verdict. This dilemma's in the book (page 67).

One story described a female doctor unwilling to tender assistance to a woman who was in the final stages of childbirth in front of a hospital. The fact that the fetus's head was protruding from the birth canal did not even prompt the physician to take action. Fearful of the possible transmission of AIDS, she insisted on waiting until a pair of rubber gloves and her instruments could be located and brought to the curbside maternity site. Then there was the complex and genealogically perplexing story of the wife who wished to use her husband's sperm to fertilize her own sister's egg. These dilemmas are in here as well, on pages 81 and 116, respectively.

Several open-ended questions were included. One of these asked participants to tell me which single trait of theirs they would bestow on their spouses if they had the power. The answers were intriguing! "Patience" led the list, followed not far behind by "extreme horniness," "talk more," "talk less," and "a better memory, as in remembering to put the toilet seat down."

I also asked the panel to tell me what they would do if they knew that the world was coming to an end in six months. "Have a child," "marry my spouse again," "quit my job," "have more sex," "love people even more," and my favorite, "max out my credit cards," were the far-and-away winners. More imaginative responses to the same question included "skydive in the nude," "go to bed with another man," "tell a guy how I really feel about him" and, from a man in Riverview, Florida, this one: "spend every penny of my money."

Asked if there was any one thing for which they might give up their lives, our respondents had these inspirational replies, followed by one of a different species and genus altogether: "anyone whom I would call friend," "another human being," "my spouse," "world peace," "to save another's life," "to uphold my way of life," and "not willingly for anything or anyone at any time."

Some respondents were positively prescient, like the woman from Baltimore, Maryland, whose suggestion for a future moral dilemma question anticipated by a year at least the premise of the Robert Redford–Demi Moore film depicting a millionaire's romp with the screen wife of Woody Harrelson. She offered this one: "If someone offered you ten million dollars to have sex with them for one night, would you do it?"

I saved the best till last. This is where respondents explained how they cheated on school tests. To qualify, they had to own up to cheating in the first place. (The techniques I learned make me wish for a second go-round in P.S. 91, P.S. 253, P.S. 234, Abraham Lincoln High School, New York University, and Adelphi University.) This glib reply takes the cake: "First, get a copy of the exam. Next, take the exam." One secret of the trade was to "write notes on my thigh and leg, covered up by a long skirt." Another offered the notion of "keeping a crib sheet in my open purse on the floor." One sneaky student would "write crib notes on the sides of my fingers. I would clench my fists whenever the teacher passed by." Then there was "use the bathroom a lot." Can anyone *really* get away with that one without a note from a urologist?

"It pays to have shifty eyes," wrote one woman from the Deep South. Another woman, this one from the southwest, supplied this masterpiece: "I could get quite a bit of information printed on my palms. No one is without sin. Hallelujah." (To which my only reply is an appreciative "Amen!")

Laurence Sterne, in *Tristram Shandy* (1761), gave the world an enduring phrase to describe a problem. "One of the two horns of my dilemma," he opined. Hobson's "*choice*" was an insoluble enigma mired in a paradox. My sticklers, though, were tough enough, especially since many of the questionnaires were completed in husband-wife households where I have no doubt that substantial debating and lobbying took place. Yet whether they pulled down the YES lever or the NO lever, all participants became winners in the philosophical sense—if perhaps not in the statistical sense. A dilemma is a dilemma is a dilemma whether it occurred in the eighteenth century or yesterday, whether it curled the eyebrows of Aristotle or Casey Stengel. We must endure what men and women have always had to endure and try to make more right choices than the other kind. Now, we must ungore ourselves and get the hell off those horns!

Mel Poretz
Merrick, New York
September 1993

WHAT WOULD YOU DO?

If you had only one choice, who would you save from death: your mate or your child?

	% SAVE MATE	% SAVE CHILD
MEN	42	58
WOMEN	19	81

Add this one to the classic Philosophy 101 posers about which came first, the chicken or the egg, and whether the glass is half full or half empty. And no cop-out, such as "I'd rescue the one closest to me," is permissible.

Women overwhelmingly responded that they would save the life of their offspring, 81 percent to 19 percent. Men opted to save their children first, but by a significantly smaller majority, 58 percent to 42 percent.

Men and women who would save their mates before their children are generally high school educated; college educations are predominant in those men and women who opted to save their children.

If you could save only one from death, would it be your mother, your father, or your mate?

	% SAVE MOTHER	% SAVE FATHER	% SAVE MATE
MEN	9	19	72
WOMEN	22	14	64

Men provided the biggest turnaround in their response to this question when stacked up against their earlier choice between their mates and their children. After declaring that they'd save their wives over their offspring 42 percent of the time, 72 percent of the men then went on to demonstrate how important these women in their lives actually are, by declaring that they'd save their wives instead of their own parents.

Women, who previously opted to save hubby in only 19 percent of the responses, would also toss the lifeline to their spouses under these new conditions—64 percent of the time.

As to who came in second, men would then drag good old Pop to safety, while women chose to pull Mom out of a burning building.

If your mate committed suicide and left a note placing blame on a family member, would you let the person named see the note, or would you hide it and its contents?

	% SHARE THE NOTE	% CONCEAL IT
MEN	22	78
WOMEN	31	69

While a distinct majority of men and women invoked the Pandora's Box Principle (it's better to keep that lid shut), more than a quarter of all respondents thought that sharing a suicide note with the affected family member would be the better thing to do.

The most poignant comment I received was this one: "It would be too much!!!" Clearly, many view the proposition as one that would only increase pain and favor suppressing such a note.

If you had the knowledge, would you inform your mate or a parent that they have an incurable disease, or would you endeavor to keep the truth from them* for as long as possible?

	% TELL	% NOT TELL
MEN	70	30
WOMEN	86	14

I s it pity, love, or a combination of the two that plays a part in the decision to tell or not to tell? More women than men (86 percent to 70 percent) declared that they would reveal the illness to a loved one. Interestingly, the older the respondents were, the more the replies indicated that those of both genders were more apt to hold off on announcing the bad news.

Is there really a *right* answer to this dilemma?

*They are in full command of their faculties.

If you interrupted a burglar in the act of robbing your home, could you shoot this person in order to protect your property? What if the intruder was threatening the life of a loved one?

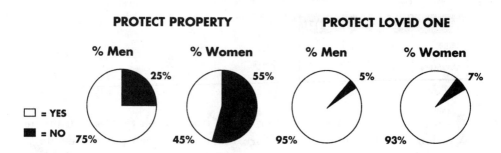

PROTECT PROPERTY

% Men

25%

75%

% Women

55%

45%

PROTECT LOVED ONE

% Men

5%

95%

% Women

7%

93%

□ = YES
■ = NO

In a world where motorists drive with locked doors and tightly rolled up windows to avoid carjackings, men registered resounding *YESSES* when it came to protecting what's theirs, to the tune of 75 percent. This positive response rate soared to a near unanimous 95 percent when it came to intervening with firearms to save the life of a loved one.

In the case of women, 45 percent would shoot to protect home and property, and that response more than doubled when it came to firing a gun in order to save the life of a loved one. The younger the woman respondent, the quicker the finger—proving that hell hath no fury like a younger woman.

You have been offered two choices in living your life over again:
(1) To start all over, but without anything elemental, such as your
looks, material wealth, skills, gender, etc., being changed.
(2) To start all over, but this time completely from scratch:
with new physical and mental characteristics and possibly a different
gender or race. Everything is different, and nothing is guaranteed!

% Men & Women Combined

35%

65%

☐ = A brand new me, please!

■ = Keep everything the same!

Practically two thirds of all respondents expressed satisfaction with the hand they were first dealt: they'd replay the same cards, thank you! Men who'd take their chances on a whole new deal came predominantly from the fifty-six-and-over category. But the female risk-takers came equally from all ages surveyed.

If there is one thing that you would give up your life for, what would that one thing be?

"**U**nknown" led the field of entries. Surprisingly, "husband/wife/spouse/mate et al." came in far behind "family" and "children." "Motherhood," "apple pie," and "flag/country" were complete no-shows. Several emphatic varieties of the "There is *nothing* I'd give my life up for" theme were heard, such as "Not willingly for anything or anyone at any time," and "You must be kidding!" (Those were two of the more printable ones in this category!) Other answers included:

For the people of the world to be happy
My God/my faith
Grandchild
World peace
A firm promise that I would go to heaven
To save the life of any of my three nephews (Lucky Huey, Louie, and Dewey!)
To save another human being

For anyone whom I would call friend
$5 million, which should go to my family
Personal freedom
My integrity
My dignity

And from a woman in Cheyenne, Wyoming: "Green peas." (I didn't know they were endangered.)

You are dying. Would you choose to expire in your sleep, or to have family and friends surround you as you peacefully, but consciously, slip away?

	% IN MY SLEEP	% WITH FRIENDS
MEN	71	29
WOMEN	77	23

Three quarters of Americans agree: An unseeing, unfeeling departure in one's sleep is ideal. Perhaps it's the case that we can't totally escape our fear of death and thus would prefer not to confront death face-on. The ones most likely to feel this way are those aged fifty-six and over.

If you had to be put to death, would you choose to die by hanging, lethal injection, electrocution, firing squad, in the gas chamber, or another way?

	% MEN	% WOMEN
HANGING	0	0
INJECTION	75	80
ELECTROCUTION	2	11
FIRING SQUAD	15	7
GAS CHAMBER	8	2
OTHER	0	0

"Hanging" and "other way" didn't get *a single vote*!!! The universal demise of choice seems to be death by lethal injection. (But will this actually help us overcome our fear of needles?) Second choice: for women, electrocution; for men, the firing squad. One wiseacre's supplemental write-in choice: "Death by nagging. It's faster."

Your elderly parent is irreversibly ill and has nothing but a lingering, painful death ahead. Would you remove any life-sustaining apparatus in order to ease your parent to a quicker, painless, and more dignified death?

S ometimes, questions such as this serve to prepare us against the time that we, unfortunately, might have to address them in actuality. It is hoped that knowing what others' actions would be, under similar circumstances, will in a small way cushion the decision that, ultimately, some of us might have to make.

Americans clearly choose to end a parent's life when the prognosis is irrefutably negative, and it is women, more than men, who would end any life-support procedures. The greatest number of women who chose this option are forty-six to fifty-five; the men holding this view are predominantly fifty-six and older.

Have you ever contemplated taking your own life? If so, did you ever attempt it?

CONTEMPLATED

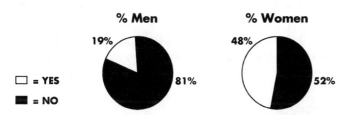

% Men

% Women

19%

81%

48%

52%

☐ = YES

■ = NO

T wo-and-a-half times more women than men acknowledged that the no-tion of suicide had intruded into their thinking at one time or another. (Note: The question did not attempt to pinpoint how old respondents were when suicide was considered.) Women in the thirty-one to forty-five bracket accounted for the highest percentage of females who thought of taking their lives. And it was men in the forty-six to fifty-five age range who, more than any other male age grouping, acknowledged having thoughts of suicide.

As to how many actually *attempted* suicide, 6 percent of men and 10 percent of women tried to take their own lives. The statistics for these attempted suicides match up for both genders with the age ranges of those who admitted having *thoughts* of suicide.

Note: In an attempt to compare the results of this question with statistics that I (erroneously) assumed suicide prevention organizations would have, I called three such groups. One "hotline" operative responded as follows:

THEM: **"Hello."**
ME: **"Suicide hotline?"**
THEM: **"Please hang on, I'll be right with you."**

You are engaged to someone who lives in a distant city, but you are physically attracted to someone who lives close by. Would you have an affair with this person, knowing that there was no chance of ever being discovered?

	% HAVE AN AFFAIR	% STAY TRUE
MEN	38	62
WOMEN	17	83

Here's a classic case of out-of-sight-out-of-your-mind or when-the-cat's-away-the-rats-will-play. Indeed, twice as many men as women would be untrue to their darlings in their fancy. Given the caveat of permanent nondiscovery, over half of the men aged eighteen to thirty (53 percent) opted to go the way of all flesh. In direct contrast to this finding, women eighteen to thirty (at 90 percent) proved the most temptation-free; it was the thirty-one to forty-five group of women (at 43 percent) who were the most inclined to let it all hang out.

If you found a credit card, would you use it for a limited time
if you were absolutely convinced that you would never get caught?

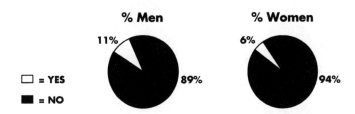

% Men

11%

89%

% Women

6%

94%

☐ = YES

■ = NO

This is a fantasy that doesn't *quite* rival the classic about being one half of a set of identical twins and being able to have your way with your sibling's spouse (see page 30), but it's an intriguing dilemma, nonetheless.

So how *do* Americans react, given this scenario? Most of us—excepting 6 percent of women and 11 percent of men—declared that when Old Man Temptation knocked, they'd slam the door in his face. Now, isn't that reassuring?

The cashier gives you change for a twenty, even though you only paid with a five-dollar bill. Do you keep the extra money or return it?

% Men & Women Combined

19%

81%

☐ = YES, KEEP THE CASH

■ = NO, RETURN IT

L et's hear it for the good guys of both sexes and not the contributor of this cop-out: "It all depends on which store it is." Really! Just about eight out of every ten respondents indicated that they would correct the cashier's error and return the excess change. One grump in the pool of respondents who opted to pocket his undeserved windfall added this comment: "It'll teach the cashier a lesson. And I'd make sure my firm never hired her in any capacity involving money." Hey . . . we all make misteaks!

Yours is a comfortable and secure family environment, complete with a loving mate, children, and financial security. If an unplanned and unsought, but passionate and overwhelming, love affair suddenly becomes possible, would you risk all for this once-in-a-lifetime grand passion?

% Men & Women Combined

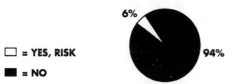

☐ = YES, RISK

■ = NO

6%

94%

Throughout this survey, women demonstrated a consistent tendency to run the good race and the long race when it came to the stability of the marriage and the family. The same holds true here: At 97 percent, women unanimously believe in looking the other way if faced with a temptation of this magnitude. Yet neither are men ready to risk all for an ephemeral period of passionate intensity: 91 percent stand by the comforts of home and hearth.

Have you ever sneaked an early peek at the ending of a gripping mystery?

	% MEN	% WOMEN
NEVER	47	32
SOMETIMES	47	57
OFTEN	6	10
ALWAYS	0	1

Virtually one out of every two male readers would have us believe that they have never ever copped a sneak at the ending of what they're reading. Only a third of women, on the other hand, claim to be totally peek-proof. As to those that *do* sneak a peek . . . sort of takes the mystery out of it all!

You have a completely identical twin. If you had the opportunity to engage in sexual relations with your twin's mate, without your true identity being discovered, would you do so?

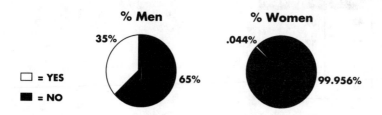

% Men

35%

65%

% Women

.044%

99.956%

□ = YES
■ = NO

Fantasies die hard, especially those of adolescence, and this one's no exception. Of the men, 35 percent leapt at the opportunity to be a component of this heady mélange. However, less than 1 percent of women panelists gave this question the time of day . . . wonder if the reason is that their brothers-in-law don't find favor in their eyes!

*If you could commit the perfect murder and never be found out
. . . would you? Whether you would or wouldn't, who would you
select to murder first?*

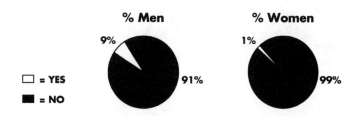

% Men

9%

91%

% Women

1%

99%

☐ = YES
■ = NO

What a relief! Americans are not a bloodthirsty breed at all—not when only 9 percent of male respondents and a microscopic 1 percent of females would opt for the satisfaction of doing somebody in without having to pay for the dastardly deed.

Leading the demographic categories for those who demurred are women aged forty-six to fifty-five and men thirty-one to forty-five. Leading the "hit" parade in the category of prime candidates for the perfect murder were:

Spouse	50%
Boss	30%
Neighbor	10%
Mother-in-law	5%
Father-in-law	3%
Teacher	2%

A number of respondents, who didn't wish to be confined to the suggested list of targets, wrote in other choices: "my neighbor's Akita," "the newspaper deliveryman who always disregards my working lawn sprinkler," and "Marty of Westport, Connecticut."

While shopping, you see someone shoplifting. Do you report the guilty party?

% Men & Women Combined

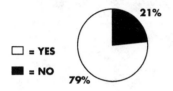

☐ = YES
■ = NO

A lmost 80 percent of both genders are disposed toward dropping the net on a shoplifter. A profile of those panelists who *wouldn't* blow the whistle finds them to be high school graduates between eighteen and thirty who earn $30,000 per year or less in blue-collar jobs.

Have you ever bought, worn, and returned a new outfit, for which you had planned, from the outset, to return it after the wearing?

% Men & Women Combined

2.5%

□ = YES
■ = NO

97.5%

Department stores on the cusp of bankruptcy can look elsewhere to plug profit leaks: Only 2 percent of men and 3 percent of women indulge in this eccentric but inexpensive way of updating their wardrobes. Perpetrators of this somewhat refined form of shoplifting generally fall in the fifty-six-and-older group.

Despite the fact that your office prohibits such actions, were you ever tempted enough to take home small articles from your office, such as pencils, Scotch tape, writing pads, and paper clips?

% Men & Women Combined

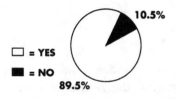

10.5%

□ = YES
■ = NO

89.5%

Everybody 'fesses up! A total of 90.5 percent of men and 88.5 percent of women bared their souls and confessed to petty larcenies. Those most likely to bring mementos home are between the ages of forty-six and fifty-five, hold college degrees, and earn between $30,000 and $50,000 annually. And where do these men and women ply their trade? You guessed it! In offices where they are predominantly managers and executives.

Have you ever taken anything from a store without paying for it, regardless of how inexpensive it was?

	% YES, TAKEN	% NO, NEVER
MEN	63	37
WOMEN	44	56

Wow! Nearly 20 percent more men than women would stick their fingers in the forbidden cookie jar! And the results go on to give new meaning to the term "white-collar crime," for those with the stickiest fingers earn their livelihoods in white-collar capacities! It's the white-collar workers who are picking the counters of variety stores clean of every tempting, tiny item that could fit into a pocket or purse. The dossier of a chain-store marauder continues to read like this: men aged forty-six to fifty-five with college degrees who make up to $50,000 annually, and women aged fifty-six and over with high school diplomas who earn $30,000 and under.

You have a chance encounter with the celebrity of your dreams.
Would you sleep with this star and experience what you're sure
will be the most satisfying sexual exchange of your life if
you had heard a rumor to the effect that the star has a
sexually communicable disease? The rumor cannot be proved
or refuted in advance of your dream date.

	% THROW CAUTION TO THE WIND	% SAFETY FIRST
MEN	18	82
WOMEN	5	95

"Safety first" and "better safe than sorry" obviously were the slogans that were uppermost in most women's minds: A mere 5 percent of them opted to risk a dubious sexual encounter, even if it was with their idol. More than three times as many men—18 percent—would take the plunge, but it's still true that a distinct majority—82 percent—would pass on the opportunity.

Who's willing to dare anything for one night of possibly unparalleled ecstasy? In terms of men: The younger (eighteen to thirty) they were, the more willing they were to throw caution to the wind and indulge their libidos. For women, the exact opposite was true: They opted for one last hurrah, with women in the fifty-six-and-over age category proving to be *two times more willing* to bed their dream celebrity than their younger counterparts.

Would you cheat on your income tax if your creative bookkeeping could never be detected?

% Men & Women Combined

46%

54%

□ = YES

■ = NO

Given a license to steal, Americans *would not hesitate* to take liberties when it comes to the dreaded due-by-April-15 paperwork. Almost half the population—47 percent of male and 45 percent of female respondents—displayed an avid eagerness to avail themselves of any loopholes they could crawl, walk, or drive through. Who's most likely to throw Uncle Sam a knuckle curve? College-educated men and high-school-educated women.

You own a business with a partner. A substantial sum of cash has unexpectedly come into your business that is impossible for anyone to detect. Would you share this windfall with your partner?

% Men & Women Combined

☐ = YES

■ = NO

5%

95%

I t's amazing how true-blue Americans can be . . . unless a basic distrust of all so-called secret questionnaires is operating here! As experience tells many of us that good partnerships are terribly difficult to come by and maintain, it is welcome indeed to discover that an average of *95 percent* of all respondents would unequivocally reveal monetary bonanzas to their partners. Only 6 percent of women and 4 percent of men would stick it to their partners with alacrity, in affirmation of the old business precept "Do unto partners before partners and their sons and their daughters and their wives do unto you!"

Given the right time, place, and opportunity, would you have an affair or even a one-nighter? What about if you were assured complete and total secrecy?

	% FLING AWAY!	% AWAY, FLING!
MEN	40	60
WOMEN	17	83

Given three out of four of the classic components for having an extramarital fling (time, place, and opportunity), 40 percent of the men were all too willing to champion this hypothetical affair. Way down on the scale were 17 percent of the women, who also admitted to having a cheating heart.

But when we added the new element of total secrecy to their decisions about extracurricular activities, women's scores jumped to show that 28 percent were suddenly willing to take a tumble between the sheets with a Mister who was not necessarily theirs. As for men, the addition of secrecy caused their score to increase by only a single percentage point. It's evident that being in harm's way does wonders for many men's libidos!

You always have been scrupulously faithful to your mate, who you now learn is having an affair. Would you engage in an affair of your own just to get even?

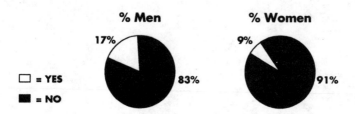

% Men

17%

83%

% Women

9%

91%

☐ = YES

■ = NO

While most wouldn't go to such an extreme, males have it two to one over females when it comes to settling the score by having a retaliatory fling. Those men who want a bite of the tail of the cat that bit them are largely of the managerial class, eighteen to thirty years of age, and earning between $30,000 and $50,000 a year. Those women who feel that revenge is the best reward are over fifty-six, college educated, and earning salaries in the $75,000 range.

You are filing a claim for a costly automobile repair with your insurance carrier, complete with a substantial medical bill covering the injuries you sustained in the accident. Do you submit the bills exactly as you receive them, or do you attempt to have them inflated in order to minimize your own costs?

	% INFLATE THE BILL	% SUBMIT ACCURATE ESTIMATE
MEN	33	67
WOMEN	47	53

Nearly half of our female respondents were likely to engage in creative bookkeeping, while only one third of our male participants would do the same. Just as with the car-scraping incident (see page 50), women proved more miserly when it comes to matters of money. Women thirty-one and over were the ones most likely to engage in this kind of imaginative claim filing, but with men, it's the youngsters between eighteen and thirty who are most likely to fiddle with the facts and fudge the figures. Now what we'd like to know is: *How many of these cons would really work?*

You owe a substantial sum to a friend who, after lending you the money on a handshake, develops Alzheimer's. No one else knows about the loan, and your friend no longer remembers the debt. Will you repay it?

% Men & Women Combined

17.5%

☐ = YES
■ = NO

82.5%

Once again, Americans demonstrate that they are an honest breed, with women at 84 percent leading the parade in acknowledging the debt to their ill benefactor. Men lag only slightly behind, at 81 percent. This means that 19 percent of men and 16 percent of women would skip out of their obligation; bear their profile in mind the next time you are tempted to lend money to someone. They are women over forty-six who earn between $30,000 and $50,000 annually and men between thirty-one and forty-five who make incomes of $75,000 and up annually. Now, as for lending money without a promissory note: Don't take the chance!

While pulling out of a parking space, you scrape the adjacent car, inflicting on it a very noticeable gash. Your own car is totally unmarked. Do you tell the owner of the parked car, who has not seen the accident occur, that you caused the damage?

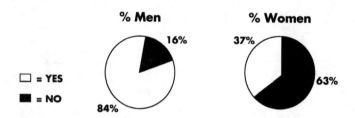

% Men

% Women

□ = YES

■ = NO

T alk about gender gaps! What happened to Mr. Tough Guy, the rough, unfeeling mug who unceremoniously and unsentimentally could be counted on to answer this question with "What they don't know won't hurt them"? Obviously, 84 percent of men today have learned to be sensitive, and so maintain that they would inform the aggrieved car owner that they damaged the Beemer. The new "tough guys" today are surely the females—all 63 percent of them, who would put the pedal to the metal and zoom away from the car-nage, never looking back and never going back, either. How to avoid taking the parking spot adjoining one of these femme-fatalistic drivers? She's college educated, fairly young (thirty-one to forty-five) and earning big bucks of $75,000 and more annually.

Your child is born one minute after midnight on January 1, thereby depriving your family of a tax deduction for the prior year. Would you claim the child as an exemption for the year just ended?

% Men & Women Combined

27.5%

□ = YES
■ = NO

72.5%

Almost three quarters of both men and women reported that they'd walk the straight and narrow on this one. But is that because of their inherent honesty, their comfortable cash flow, or their mortal fear of the IRS?

If the IRS circulated a "WANTED" poster to identify the 29 percent of men and the 26 percent of women who would fudge the forms, this is what it would look like: men with some postgrad courses, earning over $75,000 a year; women sans high school diplomas who earn an average of $50,000 annually.

Your car hits an animal—a dog, a cat, a deer. Do you stop and return to the scene of the accident? What if it was a person you hit?

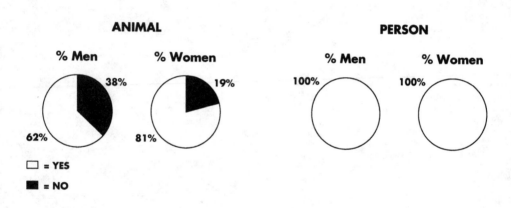

ANIMAL

% Men

38%
62%

% Women

19%
81%

PERSON

% Men

100%

% Women

100%

□ = YES
■ = NO

While everyone said he or she would return to the scene of an accident if it involved a human being, it was a different story when a four-footed critter was involved. While a goodly number of women—81 percent—would back up to see what caused that bump-thud-and-crunch, 38 percent of the men said they'd probably only take a look in the rearview mirror before stepping on the gas. Sayonara, Bambi!

You are a highly competent and professional nurse or medical technician working in a doctor's office. You realize that the doctor is about to make a serious mistake in a patient's prescription due to a misreading of the patient's chart. Do you intercede, thus risking the doctor's rebuke, or keep silent?

	% YES, INTERCEDE	% KEEP SILENT
MEN	98	2
WOMEN	99.5	0.5

In a bold and almost unanimous statement, male and female respondents agreed that saving a person's life is definitely worthy of risking a put-down from the boss. Only two out of a hundred men would permit the suspect medication to be used, and barely half a percent of the women would.

Someone you knew and thoroughly despised has died. Does this news make you genuinely happy?

	% WOULD DANCE ON THEIR GRAVE	% NOT AS BLOODTHIRSTY AS THOUGHT
TOTAL	13.5	86.5
MEN	15	85
WOMEN	12	88

The Romans may have declaimed "De mortuis, nil nisi bonum" ("Say only good things about the dead"), but obviously some of our participants don't pay much attention to history: 15 percent of the men and 12 percent of the women made no attempt to hide their pleasure at the death of someone they despised and so said "Good riddance" but not "Fare thee well."

You are a devoted fan of a major-league baseball team that is only one game away from winning the World Series. Their star left-hander, who is scheduled to pitch the deciding game, announces that he cannot because the game is being played on the day of his faith's most sacred religious holiday. What is your opinion of his decision?

	% GO PRAY!	% GO PITCH!
MEN	68	32
WOMEN	73	27

Men and women were united in their approval of the pitcher's decision to honor his god even if it meant losing a World Series. Men registered their support by 68 percent to 32 percent, women by 73 percent to 27 percent.

And after the game was played, and their favorite team lost, 98 percent of those who initially supported the pitcher's decision claimed they would *continue* to support his decision, despite the disappointing outcome.

Necessity demands that you place your very existence, your safety, and, thus, your future in the hands of a lawyer, a professional who is sworn to uphold the sanctity of your relationship. Do you fully believe that your lawyer keeps your confidences?

% Men & Women Combined

34%

☐ = YES, BELIEVE

■ = NO

66%

Read 'em and weep, counselor: 66 percent of Americans *absolutely do not believe* that their secrets are safe once deposited in a lawyer's trust! We went on to ask our participants to rank their lawyers on a scale of one to ten (with ten deserving of the highest level of trust), and here's what happened:

SCALE OF TRUST	1	2	3	4	5	6	7	8	9	10
% MEN	5	5	3	3.5	14	8	22	22	9.5	8
% WOMEN	3	1.5	6	5	19	7	12.5	20	11	14

Have you ever wished for the death of someone you hated?

% Men & Women Combined

24.5%

☐ = YES

■ = NO

75.5%

While the majority of Americans manage to put a lid on their most hostile thoughts, nevertheless they have to share space on the planet with one quarter of their fellow inhabitants who cannot. Women, to the tune of 20 percent, and men, at 29 percent, say that their lives would be immeasurably improved if the objects of their hate bought a one-way ticket to anywhere else but here.

As to those who hope that an unhappy end befalls their enemies, men of thirty-one to forty-five in blue-collar positions who earn up to $30,000 annually lead the "hit" parade. Women who share a desire for this quick fix are slightly older (forty-six to fifty-five) and earn considerably more ($75,000 per year).

Your closest friend was brutally murdered. You have been asked to press the button that will end the murderer's life. Can you bring yourself to do this?

	% BUTTON, BUTTON, WHO'S GOT THE BUTTON?	% JUST CAN'T BRING MYSELF TO DO IT . . .
MEN	80	20
WOMEN	46	54

Big disparities here when it comes to meting out retribution! Almost twice as many men as women would be able to avenge their best friends in this manner. For the record, note that those respondents most eager to press the button were college graduates earning big bucks (between $50,000 and $100,000 annually) who were in the forty-six to fifty-five age group.

Given the same circumstances as in 1945 (the chance to end a bloody war sooner rather than later), could you today give the order to drop the atomic bomb?

	% YES	% NO
MEN	75	25
WOMEN	38	62

By a ratio of two to one, more men (75 percent) than women (38 percent) would make the same fateful decision that Harry S Truman did. And it was more men from the fifty-six-plus age category who had had a closer past involvement with this tumultuous event who decisively stated that they could drop the bomb.

You are absolutely convinced that your best friend's wife is the victim of wife battering. Would you turn in the offending husband?

% Men & Women Combined

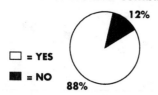

12%

☐ = YES

■ = NO

88%

The outcome to this question is reassuring. Both men and women categorically concluded that they would take the position of blowing the whistle on the wife beater. Men registered an 89 percent response compared to 87 percent for women. And it was men aged thirty-one to forty-five and women aged fifty-six and above who led the rush to batter the batterer.

It is interesting to note, however, that when it comes to a *child* who is the one being victimized (see page 76), 3 percent more men and 9 percent more women pledged to turn in the offender.

*You have been sworn in as a juror on a sensational multiple
murder case; the defendant is reputed to be a high-ranking member
of organized crime. Do you attempt, out of fear, to disqualify
yourself, or do you uphold the oath you took to try and
render an impartial verdict?*

% Men & Women Combined

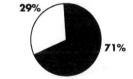

29%

71%

☐ = YES, would get out of it

■ = NO, stay and judge

The spirit of justice will triumph nearly three quarters of the time, according to our results. Once impaneled, 70 percent of men and 72 percent of women declared that they would take and maintain their seats in the jury box, regardless of the possible outcome. Holders of college degrees were among those most likely to be unswerving in their decision to judge the case without regard to the defendant's reputation. Age-wise, younger women (eighteen to thirty) and older men (fifty-six and over) formed the nucleus of those who staunchly defended the principle of trial by jury.

A world-class runner, you are close to achieving international fame and fortune. But now you are offered steroids that assuredly can improve your performance. The downside is that you might end up crippled later in life. Do you take the steroids and the subsequent pot of gold, or do you reach for the best you can do without them?

	% TAKE THE DRUGS	% DO MY BEST ON MY OWN
MEN	3.5	96.5
WOMEN	1	99

From this side of the starting line, panelists were virtually unanimous in reaching the conclusion that performance enhancers, which captured numerous international track and field stars in their thrall, are just not worth the risk: 96.5 percent of the male and 99 percent of the female participants returned landslide votes *against* steroids.

You give your time and money to support hostels for the homeless and hospices for the terminally ill. But now, one of them has announced its intention to occupy a building around the corner from your home. Do you now support or oppose this plan?

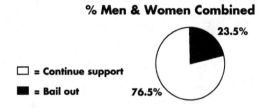

% Men & Women Combined

□ = Continue support

■ = Bail out

23.5%

76.5%

Most Americans, we're pleased to say, are not hypocrites! Just over three quarters of those who participated in our poll would maintain their support, in contrast to the 23.5 percent of those who would withdraw theirs now that the object of their onetime affection is moving in with them, as it were. Men with postgraduate credits and women who never finished high school were those most likely to support the cause of hostels and hospices, regardless of where they are situated.

There comes a time in most doctor-patient relationships when a patient feels that a second or third opinion might be advisable and in his/her own best interest. Have you ever felt that you wanted to get a second opinion but failed to follow through on that urge because you feared that your request might adversely affect your relationship with your doctor?

The majority—three quarters—of Americans *will* risk alienating their doctors when their own health is on the line. But 23 percent of male patients and 25 percent of female patients do back off from seeking a second opinion because of their concern that their doctor might view their decision as a sign of diminished confidence. But what actually happened when said patients went on to obtain second opinions? Were their fears realized? Did their physicians then turn on them?

So we asked: *Did your relationship with your primary doctor deteriorate because you sought a second opinion?*

Yes, indeed, said 18 percent of women and 31 percent of male patients, who went on to refer to these doctors as "dictators," "having a deity complex," and "being definitely not a people person."

We then asked: *Just how much confidence do you have in your doctor?*

On a scale of one to ten (with ten being deserving of the most trust), only 10 percent of men rated their doctors a perfect ten. However, 27 percent of women were ready to put their physicians on the highest pedestal. The following chart shows the range of doctor-patient relationships.

SCALE OF TRUST	1	2	3	4	5	6	7	8	9	10
% MEN	0	0	2	3	5	8	11	29	32	10
% WOMEN	0	4	0	1	7	6	13	28	14	27

Would you report a child molester . . . even if the suspect is your best friend? What about a relative? A respected church leader?

% Men & Women Combined

5%

☐ = YES

■ = NO

95%

This turned out to be more of a no-brainer than a mind-boggler, with women meting out the harshest verdicts across the board: 96 percent of females would turn in their friend; 94 percent of males would do the same. When we asked if they would alter that decision in the event that the suspect were *a relative*, men remained unswerving in their response, but 3 percent more women (99 percent) would turn in the offender.

Men mellowed slightly when we asked how they'd handle *a respected church leader* (minister, rabbi, priest, etc.) whom they caught. Two percent less—92 percent—would blow the whistle, whereas women's scores stayed at 99 percent.

Have you ever cheated in a card game played for money?

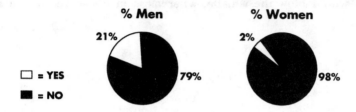

% Men

21%

79%

% Women

2%

98%

☐ = YES

■ = NO

Before your next friendly little game starts, put aside the chips and dips and take inventory of your comrades. Knowing who you're playing with might assure you of a fair shuffle and keep you in the chips (the red, white, and blue kind). A 21 percentage of male respondents admitted to playing somewhat fast and loose at least once, with left-handers heading the list of these slick cardsters. Typical male cardsharks earn less than $30,000 annually, are on the young side (aged eighteen to thirty), and have only a modicum of high school and college diplomas among them.

And what kind of deal do women give themselves on this hand? Not enough women admitted to playing cards or cheating to paint a specific picture, but of the minuscule 2 percent who responded affirmatively, they are over forty-six years of age and, like the male players, have a minimum of formal education.

As a juror, you have sworn not to discuss the case with anyone until the verdict has been reached and the trial is officially over. Do you faithfully observe this oath to the letter, or do you share the details of the trial with others?

	% BLABBERMOUTH	% CLOSED MOUTH
MEN	73	27
WOMEN	61	39

Only two thirds of our citizens can be counted on to keep their mouths zipped while a trial is still in progress. And it is women who are more likely than men to keep mum. The blabbermouth females are bunched in the forty-six to fifty-five age grouping and have some college education to go along with their salary, which reaches a max of $30,000 per annum. Men who might be expected to live up to their oaths are in the same age bracket, but earn $50,000 to $75,000 per year.

You are a physician. A taxicab has just pulled over with a woman passenger in an advanced stage of labor. You instinctively pitch in to help, until you realize you do not have your protective rubber gloves or any other medical equipment with you. Would you withhold your help until the equipment arrived in order to ensure that you will not be exposed to any communicable disease?

	% PITCH IN	% BUTT OUT
MEN	88	12
WOMEN	93	7

When nature calls, duty isn't far behind. Only 7 percent of all women polled would stand aside and let nature take its course until a pair of rubber gloves arrived. A whopping 93 percent said they would disregard their own welfare to assist the unborn child and the mother; 12 percent of men would make the hands-off choice. The real dilemma here is this: Now that we know what mere citizens would do, what would the *medicos* actually do? If we weren't sure that we'd receive a bill from them in exchange for their filling out a survey questionnaire, we'd ask!

Note: According to an April 1992 news report in the *New York Times* about an identical incident, the physician chose to wait for the arrival of her rubber gloves and other equipment. By the time they arrived, the mother had delivered the baby unaided.

Having received notice of jury duty, you are advised that the case for which you might be impaneled could go on for months. Do you do anything and everything possible in order to be excused, or do you simply go and take your chances?

	% EXCUSE ME!	% I'LL STICK AROUND
MEN	47	53
WOMEN	35	65

One third of our female respondents indicated that they would seek out each and every loophole in the hope that they would not be seated a trial of indeterminate duration. Nearly half of our male panelists would also choose this route to escape the courtroom. Upper-income earners (men making $75,000 and over, women earning between $50,000 and $75,000 annually) who might think they're too indispensable to their jobs were the ones most likely to lead the flight out of the halls of justice.

Plato posited this one: Is it better to suffer injustice at the hands of others or to be unjust toward them?

	% SUFFER	% BE UNJUST FIRST
MEN	81	19
WOMEN	89	11

What this boils down to is this: Should you let others do unto you, or would you prefer to do unto others first? The results speak volumes about our preference for suffering the slings instead of loosing the arrows! 81 percent of men and 89 percent of women bought into this Platonic concept. Of those who said they would rather slap than turn the other cheek, it was those in the thirty-one to forty-five age category who leaned to the first-strike philosophy.

According to national studies, less than 10 percent of all female rape victims actually report the incident to the police. If you became a victim of rape, would you be one of the vocal 10 percent or one of the silent 90 percent?

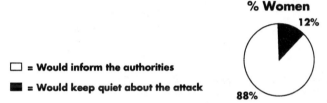

% Women

12%

□ = **Would inform the authorities**

■ = **Would keep quiet about the attack**

88%

S eems there's a new spin on the stats, cited above, if the women responding to our survey are an accurate barometer of things to come. Over 88 percent of our female respondents declared they'd be more than happy to do their part in helping the authorities get rapists off the streets: They'd report the incident.

A profile of the woman who, for whatever her reasons, would *not* file a complaint contains these commonalities: She has earned a postgraduate degree, has an annual income between $30,000 and $50,000, and is over fifty-six years of age. Women who *would* file charges generally fall into these categories: They have high school diplomas and many have some college education, they earn an average of $50,000 per year, and they range from thirty-one to fifty-five years of age.

The short story "The Devil and Daniel Webster" and the musical comedy Damn Yankees *are based on the Faust legend wherein the devil offers long years of success and fortune in exchange for eternal possession of one's soul. If you were offered such a deal, would you accept it or turn it down?*

% Men & Women Combined

6%

94%

☐ = YES, DEALS WITH THE DEVIL

■ = NO DEAL!

Women, traditionally credited with possessing more sales resistance than men, are not buying this pitch *at all*. Less than 4 percent would go for the buzz today and the hangover tomorrow. Surprisingly, female executives making a quite sizable annual salary of $75,000 or more headed up the meager contingent of women who would most likely play hardball with Beelzebub.

Two times as many men (8 percent) as women would sign on the bottom line. In stark contrast to the income of those females who chose a satanic alliance, the earning level for men was largely in the lowest-income category—$30,000 and under—which might account for their susceptibility to a deal that would materially reward them.

You are in a restaurant rest room, and you notice an employee leaving without washing his/her hands. Do you bring the matter to the attention of the proprietor? If so, do you do so publicly or privately?

Three questions, probably more to the point than those above, are these: Would you finish your meal? Would you pay your check? and Would you *ever* go back to that restaurant?

Respondents to the basic question split the pie right down the middle: 52.9 percent of both genders would definitely have a tête-à-tête with the restaurateur. That means the other half would simply swallow their revulsion. And almost all of the 50-plus percent who *would* confront the establishment's management would do it sub rosa. Only a token 2 percent of male protesters and less than 1 percent of women would make a scene in public.

Your father-in-law is foreign-born, and you have just learned that he has been, and is, an agent of long standing for an unfriendly world power. Do you report him to the authorities?

	% TURN HIM IN	% KEEP HIS SECRET
MEN	48	52
WOMEN	42	58

A measure of what our panelists think about their fathers-in-law reveals itself in the bottom line of this mind-bender. Just about half of our male participants thought their wives' fathers should be tossed into the jug. Women rallied slightly more when it came to protecting their fathers-in-law, to the tune of 58 percent. Only 42 percent of them would protect their country by denouncing the family spy.

If you are caught so much as looking at a classmate's test paper, it is your classmate, not you, who will fail the test. You need a good grade desperately. Would you put your classmate at risk by attempting to copy his/her paper?

	% SNEAK A PEEK	% KEEP EYES GLUED TO MY OWN PAPER
MEN	5	95
WOMEN	13	87

Males played it safe, refusing to enter this potentially explosive minefield. In only 5 percent of their responses did they indicate that they'd take a stroll on the wild side. Showing a more feisty . . . and less ethical spirit, 13 percent of females would grab for the better grade, despite the painful consequences—to someone else!

Without your permission, a former friend has given your name as a character reference. The friend in question is qualified, but you no longer like this person. Do you give the applicant a thumbs-up . . . or a negative reference because of your personal feelings?

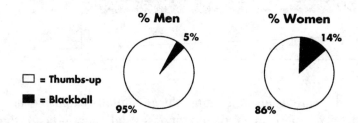

% Men

5%

95%

% Women

14%

86%

☐ = Thumbs-up

■ = Blackball

Only 5 percent of men would blackball the candidate, but almost triple that amount of women—14 percent—would put the kiss of the spiteful woman on the onetime friend. Men in executive and management positions gave a negative reference 9 percent of the time. Women employed in blue-collar capacities would nix an ex-buddy to the tune of an astonishing 22 percent. Still, all in all, the numbers are rather low, revealing that Americans can block out their feelings and maintain an objective posture if need be. *And* if they *want* to!

Would you tell a perfect stranger that his/her fly was open? How about a friend of the same gender? A friend of the opposite gender?

	TELL A STRANGER		TELL A FRIEND OF SAME GENDER		TELL A FRIEND OF OPPOSITE GENDER	
	% YES	% NO	% YES	% NO	% YES	% NO
MEN	78	22	100	0	83	17
WOMEN	36	64	95	5	89	11

Twice as many men as women would gallop to the rescue of an unknown human being. And every single man polled declared, in chorus, that they would tell a *male* buddy that his zipper wasn't zipped. While not exactly unanimous, a hefty 95 percent of women (59 percent more than their response to the generic, stranger question) told us that they would render the good deed so long as the recipient of their largesse was a *female* friend.

But the tables turned somewhat on friends of the opposite sex. For the first time, more women (89 percent) than men (83 percent) would rush to the rescue. Why the decrease in the male response? Is it pure embarrassment on their part or a lack of recognition that the situation can be just as mortifying for females? Go figure . . . we can't!

Circumstances beyond your control require that you remarry your spouse, assuming you are willing to do so. If you choose not to do so, there will be no recriminations whatsoever. What is your choice?

	% I RE-DO	% I RE-DO NOT
MEN	76	24
WOMEN	69	31

Three quarters of the men polled were willing to say, "I did and I do." The older segments of the male age spectrum—notably those between forty-six and fifty-five years of age—were most willing to commit themselves again.

Only 69 percent of women polled were eager to take that second walk down the aisle. Of these, over half were in the youngest bracket—that is, the under-thirty-somethings.

If you could transfer to your mate the one trait that you possess that you wish your mate possessed, which one would it be?

The answers, by and large, followed two tracks, one positive and one negative. A positive one is typified by "greater sensitivity" or "be more creative." Negative responses included "remember to put down the toilet seat and lid" and "that he not lie." Favorites abound, but especially this one: "No mate, thank God!" "Patience" led the list, with "neatness" not far behind (got that, Oscar Madison?). Some other popular choices are these:

A sense of fiscal responsibility
To get him to cut down on cussing
Not to worry about things you can't control
My sense of humor
Horniness (also: more sexually active)
Generosity
Trust

A better memory
Common sense
An even temper
My religious beliefs
Frugality (also: the ability to save money)
Intelligence
Tolerance
The ability to forgive
To be less selfish
To talk more
To talk less
To be more romantic

You, your spouse, and a couple of neighborhood friends are watching a pornographic video when you suddenly realize that you are the only one who recognizes that its star is the daughter of some neighbors. Do you spill the beans?

	% YES	% NO
MEN	41	59
WOMEN	56	44

But of course! say the women (56 percent); but when it comes to the guys, it's absolutely not (59 percent)! Unfortunately, we didn't ask our respondents if, after imparting the stunning revelation, they completed their viewing of the video or rushed to telephones and fax machines to enlighten the entire neighborhood.

A friend asks for your opinion about an original piece of literature or a newly complete painting. You think the material is absolutely dreadful.

Do You: ☞ *Lie about it?*

☞ *Diplomatically tone down your true feelings?*

☞ *Tell the complete and utter truth?*

	% LIE THROUGH OUR TEETH	% BE DIPLOMATIC ABOUT IT	% TELL THE UN-VARNISHED TRUTH
MEN	2	76	22
WOMEN	6	85	9

Only 9 percent of women would tell the truth . . . but over twice that many men (22 percent) would. However, most (85 percent of women and 76 percent of men) would employ their diplomatic skills when the moment of "truth" arrived. Only 2 percent of men said they'd lie outright as their way of avoiding this hurdle—one-third the tally of women who'd lie rather than deliver the awful truth.

You and your mate have learned that your unborn child will be born so profoundly deformed that its postpartum life will be extremely short and painful. Do you permit the fetus to develop until term, or do you abort the fetus now so that whichever organs are viable might be transplanted in an attempt to save the lives of other newborns?

A supersensitive issue here, and there isn't any right answer. The option of giving organs to those newborns in dire need of them did attract a substantial majority, however: 87.8 percent of men and 80 percent of women. The ages of men who dominated their gender's response were, first, those aged fifty-six and over, followed closely by men thirty-one to forty-five. Women in favor of this gift of life were forty-six to fifty-five, closely followed by those thirty-one to forty-five.

Your mate is an elementary school teacher who you now learn has been sexually molesting his pupils. Do you take steps to somehow end this practice, or do you ignore it, letting matters take their own course?

% Men & Women Combined

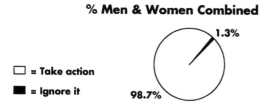

1.3%

☐ = Take action
■ = Ignore it

98.7%

American men and women, to the tune of 98.4 percent and 99 percent respectively, believe in preemptive action. They would not rely on time or anything or anyone else to eventually resolve matters one way or the other. That's absolutely wonderful!

Your job makes you privy to the fact that your company is illegally dumping toxic material. The usual kind of anonymous tip to the authorities is unlikely to produce any positive results. Would you risk your job by bringing the actions of your firm to the attention of the authorities?

	% RISK IT!	% PLAY IT SAFE!
MEN	75	25
WOMEN	83	17

Maybe it was the example of Karen Silkwood's heroism . . . or maybe women simply do not relish the prospect of seeing their offspring glow in the dark! Whatever the reason for their heightened sensitivity in this particular area, women were more vocal about putting their jobs on the line to stop the pollution of our environment. They registered a powerful 83 percent on the antipollution scale. The male panel also clearly agreed, although not quite as strongly as women, to the tune of 75 percent. A profile of these valorous women shows that they are generally over fifty-six, college educated, and work in executive capacities, earning from $30,000 to $50,000 per year.

A letter addressed to your mate is clearly marked "extremely confidential . . . for your eyes only." Do you steam it open, read it, and then reseal it?

	% PUTTING THE KETTLE ON!	% PATIENCE IS A VIRTUE . . .
MEN	1.5	98.5
WOMEN	29	71

The clear and present fact is that a mere 1.5 percent of men would own up to engaging in postal espionage, while women would steam, read, and seal in 29 percent of their responses. (Yes, we double-checked the statistics!) So, men, better be careful about giving out your home address!

Can you trust your mate with your deepest, darkest, most important secret?

	% YES	% NO
MEN	64	36
WOMEN	74	26

More women (74 percent) plighted their troth, as well as their trust, in their mates than did the opposite gender. Men lagged 10 percent behind in maintaining a clean slate with their spouses. Men least likely to believe in their wives' abilities to keep a secret have postgraduate degrees, earn in excess of $75,000 annually, and are over fifty-six years of age. Confidantes who can't keep confidences! What are marriages coming to? (And what does everyone have to *hide?*)

Your two-year-old child is rescued from death, but has suffered irreversible brain damage. Can you bring yourself to at least think that you would have preferred the child to have died?

	% YES	% NO
MEN	71	29
WOMEN	80	20

Eight out of ten women were able to express the wish that perhaps the child might have been better off had it perished. They were supported in this devastating Hobson's choice by 71 percent of the male respondents. The younger they were, the more decisively women and men voted for a quick end. Respondents entering and passing middle age staunchly voted for the future . . . any kind of future . . . for the stricken child.

Your public library has been hounding you for a book that you insist you returned. Now you discover the book in your home. Do you return it and take your medicine, or do you stonewall despite continuing notices from the library?

	% TAKE IT BACK	% BURY IT
MEN	65	35
WOMEN	50	50

rivial, you say? Trivial, indeed! It's far from insignificant to the 65 percent of American men who would march into the library and cough up the book and the whopping fine that goes with it! The women are equally divided as to their actions. Some would cleanse their consciences, while others would choose to let the book, like auld acquaintances, be forgotten.

Would you insist that your unmarried daughter obtain an abortion if she became pregnant by a man of a different race?

% Men & Women Combined

14.5%

☐ = YES

■ = NO

85.5%

America, you've come a long way! Solid majorities of both women and men (86 percent and 85 percent, respectively) affirmed that a "hands-off" attitude is the best one to take. Who were the ones who expressed the minority opinion? Women between forty-six and fifty-five whose incomes topped $50,000, and men between eighteen and thirty whose incomes ran between $30,000 and $50,000 yearly.

Your child has become engaged to someone of a different race. Would you seek to break their engagement for that reason?

% Men & Women Combined

□ = YES, interfere

■ = NO, leave them alone

20.5%

79.5%

Despite a large number of supporters on the side of letting their child make his or her own choice, 24 percent of men and 17 percent of women would provoke another *West Side Story* by interfering. Consistent with the attitudes expressed on the previous question, those who would try to separate the lovers are led by women aged forty-six to fifty-five and men aged eighteen to thirty. This time, however, both genders earned between $30,000 and $50,000 annually.

You've learned that your child has participated in a larceny.
Will you inform the authorities?

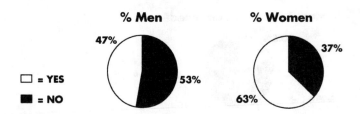

% Men   % Women

47%   37%

53%   63%

☐ = YES
■ = NO

Quite a few more women than men—63 percent versus 47 percent—would turn their children in and make them face up to their responsibilities. Interestingly, it's females eighteen to thirty who predominantly support this viewpoint. These women, generally, hold college diplomas and earn upward of $50,000 a year. The law-and-order males come from two age brackets for the most part: forty-six to fifty-five, and fifty-six and over. Men *least* likely to blow the whistle on their progeny tend to be high school graduates earning an average of $40,000 annually.

If you had the power to start the parenthood phase of your life all over again, would you restart with the same children, or would you prefer different ones?

	% KEEP THE KIDS	% TRADE 'EM IN
MEN	92	8
WOMEN	94	6

Eight percent of men would declare: "Honey, I swapped the kids!" And only 6 percent of women would opt for a clean slate. Who's most likely to swap? They'd be men thirty-one to forty-five who earn $30,000 or less a year and women fifty-six and over.

All in all, it's comforting to know that the unconditional nature of a parent's love still holds true. We love our kids just as they are, flaws and all.

Given that the world is going to come to an end in six months, what one thing would you do for the very first time?

Give more of my inner self
Have an affair with "him" or "her"
Fly (does not stipulate whether it's "learn to fly," "be flown," or "keep mine zipped" [see page 94])
Seduce a certain young man whom I think is attracted to me
Skydive (both clothed and in the buff)
Quit my job and tell my boss off, but good!
Have a baby (if I could accomplish it in six months)!
Pray
Spend every damn nickel I own
Have a mistress
Go to bed with a different man every night for six straight months
Go to bed with another man
Tell this guy how I really feel about him

The above notwithstanding, the two most popular responses turned out to be "Don't know" and "Never thought of it before." Different, and therefore worthy of separate mention, was this variant: "Don't care and don't give a damn!"

Given that the world is going to come to an end in six months, what one thing would you do again?

There was no clear-cut winner in this field of wannado's and wannabe's. Sentimentally, one entry stood alone as a moving statement, the only one in this vein: "Marry my wife." "Extravagant spending" was much favored, as was "travel." There were even a couple of votes for "Get roaring drunk on the last day of the sixth month." Winner of the get-to-the-point award is this one: "If I were a *young* woman again, I could really answer this one!" Other highlights:

Max out my credit cards
Rededicate myself to God
Take the family to Disney World
Tell someone I love him
Relive all the happy moments
Go elk hunting
Love people more
Drink, gamble, and have sex (Editor's note: by unanimous decision, we regard this
    as meeting the criterion of one single choice)

Would you permit your husband to donate sperm to a woman who would remain permanently anonymous? What if your own sister* were to be the recipient?

| | % ANONYMOUS | | % DONATION TO SISTER | |
	YES	NO	YES	NO
WOMEN	44	56	38	62

Forty-four percent of women would permit their husbands to artificially inseminate an unknown woman's egg. As in the question that deals with surrogacy (see page 118), the youngest group in the survey, women between eighteen and thirty, felt most strongly about allowing their husbands to participate in this set of circumstances.

On the question of using their husbands' sperm to fertilize the eggs of

*Her husband's sperm, for whatever reason, is not able to fertilize her egg.

their own sisters, *fewer* women (38 percent) voted in favor of this highly charged issue, showing a preference for the fertilization of a total stranger! One reason might be the convoluted relationships that such a union can create. A male child, for example, would be both a son and nephew to the donor and a step-son and nephew to the wife of the donor, giving new meaning to the old conundrum "I'm My Own Grandpa." And perhaps wives might be fearful of the bond that would be forged between sister and husband!

Could you serve as surrogate mother for your own sister, using her own egg and her own husband's sperm?

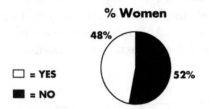

% Women

48%

52%

☐ = YES

■ = NO

What an evenly divided issue: 48 percent of women would do all in the name of sisterly love and become a surrogate mother, while 52 percent could not and would not go to such lengths! Within the youngest segment of women (eighteen to thirty), 55 percent supported such surrogacy, while 57 percent of women aged thirty-one to forty-five expressed an opposition to it.

We also asked the men to put themselves in this situation hypothetically.

The male vote went 40 percent in favor of surrogacy and a convincing 60 percent against. Heavily in support of surrogacy were men aged fifty-six and over; unlike their female counterparts, those in the eighteen to thirty group tended to reject such an idea.

Do you do anything about someone who has sneaked into a long movie line in which you have been waiting? (Do not take any "fudge" factor into consideration—such as the size, gender, or number of tattoos of the line-breaker.)

Men, more than women, will protect their turf, yet for both genders, a majority *would* take the offensive. More than three quarters of men (76 percent) would protest unwarranted incursion in the line and 65 percent of women would do the same. Their comments indicated that they fumed and fussed *more* when their wives and girlfriends (or husbands and boyfriends) were on line to witness their bravado.

How do you react to people who talk loudly while the movie is playing?

	% "SHHHH"	% PROTEST OUT LOUD	% SUFFER IN SILENCE
MEN	78	17	5
WOMEN	70	15	15

You accidentally come across your teenager's diary. If you choose to, you can read it without anyone ever knowing. Do you? What if it were your spouse's?

| | TEEN'S DIARY | | SPOUSE'S DIARY | |
	% TO PEEK	% . . . OR NOT TO PEEK	% TO PEEK	% . . . OR NOT TO PEEK
MEN	34	66	47	53
WOMEN	58	42	54	46

More women (58 percent) than men (34 percent) would whip out their specs and enjoy a good read at the expense—or, who knows? perhaps the benefit—of their teenaged child. But when we asked the men if they would read a diary penned by their *wives*, their results soared, to a high of 47 percent. The majority of women (54 percent) remained ready and willing to sneak a peek at their husbands' journals. So, here's what we've learned about diaries: Half or even more of women will read *any* diary they can get their hands on! A mere third of men have their curiosities ignited by invading their children's innermost written thoughts, but that curiosity grows when it comes to prying into their wives' private musings.

If your best friend asked you what you really thought of him or her, would you be frank or diplomatic? (Your friend has vigorously requested that you be completely objective and honest.)

	% WOULD TAKE OUR BEST SHOT	% WOULD MAKE SURE IT WOULD BE BLANKS!
MEN	77	23
WOMEN	74	26

Seventy-five percent of our respondents would put their friendships on the line and tell it like it is. Too bad we aren't able to tally all the egos that have been bruised and all the umbrages and offenses that have been taken, in the name of the "I-cannot-tell-a-lie" shtick. ("Honest, Abe, I truthfully don't think too many people are going to understand that part about four-score-and-seven.")

Have you ever displayed in your home a hated, ugly, and useless gift just because the donor happened to be paying you a visit?

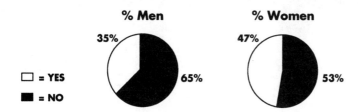

M ovie and sit-com scenarios have been created around Carole Lombard or "Lucy Ricardo" driving husbands Robert Montgomery or "Ricky Ricardo" to the brink of panic. Why? Because they couldn't remember where they had concealed the hand-painted ivory carving of an eggplant, and elderly Aunt Matilda, the donor, is due to arrive in fifteen minutes. "We don't want to hurt the old dear's feelings, do we?"

Count on almost half of females—47 percent—to showcase the eggplant, as ugly as that thing may be. But 65 percent of males hate the eggplant enough to keep it buried, Auntie M's sensibilities and possibly generous bequest notwithstanding.

After an all-out fight with your spouse, do you then forgive and forget . . . or do you first look to get even?

% Men & Women Combined

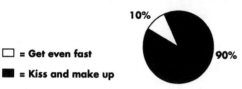

□ = Get even fast

■ = Kiss and make up

10%

90%

A Roman ruler once declared that forgiveness is better than revenge. But what did this togaed tyrant know about an old-fashioned knock-down-and-drag-out marital melee? Ten percent of our respondents declared that they wanted one more swipe at the jugular, with 14 percent of the women and 6 percent of the men not wanting to bury the past or the hatchet quite so readily.

Women who are slow to cool off are high school graduates with some college who earn between $30,000 and $50,000 and are aged eighteen to forty-five. Those males who have postgrad degrees or credits, are in the over $75,000 income category, and are forty-six years of age and older would be most apt to let bygones be bygones.

Your teenager drives home one night with a substantial dent in the fender of the family car. In the morning you learn a serious, but nonfatal, hit-and-run accident occurred in your neighborhood the previous night. Would you try to find out from your youngster if he or she was involved? Would you notify the authorities if your teen was the driver in the accident? What if your child was responsible for a death in the hit-and-run?

More women than men (94 percent to 85 percent) would want to uncover the *truth*—even if it wasn't so pretty. Who would want to know it the most? Men and women aged thirty-one to forty-five who earn up to $30,000 annually.

As to how a parent would deal with the knowledge of his or her son's or daughter's involvement in the hit-and-run, once again, women led, at 88 percent, in averring that they would bring the matter to the attention of the authorities. Men weren't far behind, at 84 percent.

The third part of this question was really loaded! We asked what our respondents would do if their teenager's involvement caused a death. In this scenario, 88 percent of men but only 81 percent of women declared that they would notify the police, despite the toll it would take on the youngster and the entire family. How would *you* deal with this awesome dilemma?

A congressional report declares that one in seven married women has been raped by her own husband. If this happened to you, would you report it? What if it happened again? How many times would it take?

Only 56 percent of the women polled would report their husbands if they raped them. These whistle blowers are high school educated, fifty-six years of age and over, and have a yearly income of up to $30,000. As to the minority who would not file a complaint with the police, many explained their stance by saying that instead of reporting it, they would leave him; or that if it just happened "once in a blue moon," they wouldn't call in the police.

And, indeed, when queried as to whether they would report a rape if it happened again, there *was* a dramatic increase in police notification—up some twenty percentage points, to 76 percent. Those who told us they would leap to take action under these circumstances are mostly college-educated women, aged eighteen to thirty, with salaries in the $50,000 to $75,000 range. One respondent declined to stipulate the point at which her forbearance and her husband's bestiality would cross the line. She said: "It would depend on the amount of the violence."

When asked to speculate on how many times a spouse-rape would have to happen before the wife cried "Enough!" the participants responded as follows:

FREQUENCY	1x	2x	3x	4x	5x	6x	7x	8x	9x	10x and above
PERCENTAGE	56	22	10	6	—	—	—	—	2	4

Would you remain in a marriage if you found out that your mate had had one extramarital relationship? What if it had happened more than once?

| | ONCE IS ENOUGH | | TWICE IS NOT NICE | |
	% STAY	% LEAVE	% STAY	% LEAVE
MEN	61	39	31	71
WOMEN	73	27	16	84

Women turn out to be not only more compassionate, but they're more forgiving, too. Whereas 39 percent of men would pull the plug on a marriage upon learning of only one affair by their mates, 73 percent of the women would endure and keep the ship on course. But watch out for the shoals ahead because when we asked the same group what they would do if they found out that there had been *multiple* affairs, it became necessary to batten down the hatches and break out the heavy weather gear! The men, who previously scored 61 percent for riding out the first storm, dropped that munificent number like a falling barometer and weighed in with a vote of 71 percent to abandon ship. The women, of whom 73 percent would grin and bear one transgression, virtually wiped their hands of any marriage that produced a two-timing two-timer. Only *16* percent would be willing to stay with the ship.

For those who *wouldn't* pull the trigger after a single indiscretion or even two, we asked them how many times would it take before they'd decide to scuttle the love boat and their philandering partner?

Here's what happened:

NUMBER OF TIMES:	1 or 2	3	4	5	6	7	8	9	10 or more
MEN	71	15	3	2	0	0	0	0	9
WOMEN	84	5	3	4	2	1	0	0	1

If you had absolute, irrefutable proof, would you tell your best friend that his/her mate was having an affair?

	% TELL	% KEEP LIPS CLAMPED SHUT
MEN	40	60
WOMEN	47	53

Nope! Most wouldn't. As for those who would trip over their running shoes to get to their friends—40 percent of men and 47 percent of women—they obviously believe in such homilies as silence ain't golden and ignorance is not bliss! Maybe the real soul-searcher here is this: Would *we* want to be told by our best friends (or any friend, for that matter) that *our* soul mate is really a heel?

One respondent added: "My best friend's husband made a pass at me and I never told her. She had enough pain living with the jerk. Now, he's long gone, and we are still best friends."

An important telephone conversation is taking place in another room of your home, and your mate has not invited you to listen in on the call. On the other hand, you have not been requested to refrain from doing so. Do you listen in?

	% YES	% NO
MEN	11	89
WOMEN	26	74

More than twice as many women as men would assume the listening position, placing their palm over the mouthpiece to muffle their labored breathing and conceal a telltale cough or sneeze. Yet these are *still* small percentages. In fact, 89 percent of the guys wouldn't pick up the phone (or so they claim!), and 74 percent of the gals also claim to favor the what-you-don't-know-won't-hurt-you school of thought.

Your newborn child is sickly and unlikely to live beyond a few years at most. If you could substitute your baby for somebody else's perfectly healthy newborn baby, would you do it? (Your action would never be detected.)

% Men & Women Combined

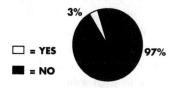

3%

☐ = YES
■ = NO

97%

Despite the frequency with which we read of real-life baby-switching in hospital nurseries, virtually all of the respondents would raise their biological offspring despite the emotional and financial tolls such a moral decision would entail. Only 3.5 percent of women and 2.5 percent of men would wreak havoc on another family's life and make such a big switch.

Your once idyllic marriage has gone sour. Do you end it, or do you continue, unhappy as you are, for the sake of the children, who are still in preschool? What about if the kids are elementary school age? High schoolers or in college?

Women's consistent position through all three phases of this question is that, *if it's broken, don't bother to fix it*—especially once the children are older. While 54 percent of mothers would end the marriage even if the children were under five years of age, 64 percent would bid adieu to a relationship that had gone sour while the children were in elementary school, and 73 percent are all for moving on once their offspring are in high school or college.

Men, surprisingly, produced more conservative results in all three segments of this difficult question. Only 32 percent of fathers would hit the road and never come back if preschoolers were still romping from room to room;

that number decreased by 2 percent when elementary school children were involved. The big surprise is that *less than half* (44 percent) would turn on their heels once the kids were safely tucked away in high school or college! Where's *your* head and heart on this one?!

A person you have never seen before leaves a public rest room, trailing a length of toilet paper from their clothing. Do you do anything to short-circuit this person's inevitable embarrassment?

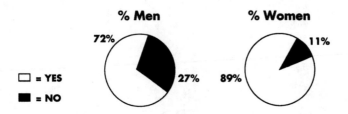

% Men

72%

27%

% Women

11%

89%

□ = YES
■ = NO

I t's *Ms.* Galahad, broadsword in hand, who is most likely to rush to the rescue. Of women, 89 percent would charge into action to rescue the errant man or maid; that's a response that's 17 percent higher than the male response. The youngest and oldest groups of women showed the least enthusiasm for the mission, while the middle group—those aged thirty-one to fifty-five—proved the most eager to save the day. With men, it's those thirty-one and over who are the quickest to help out.

Demographics

Participants in our survey represented a broad cross section of Americans and came from all fifty states. The following are some characteristics of our respondents.

GENDER	
MALE	**51%**
FEMALE	**49%**

AGE	
18–30	**22%**
31–45	**29%**
46–55	**26%**
56 AND OVER	**23%**

ANNUAL INCOME	
UNDER $30,000	**44%**
$30,000–50,000	**27%**
$51,000–75,000	**20%**
OVER $75,000	**9%**

EDUCATION	
SOME HIGH SCHOOL	5%
HIGH SCHOOL GRADUATES	34%
SOME COLLEGE	26%
COLLEGE DEGREE	16%
SOME POSTGRAD	11%
POSTGRADUATE DEGREE	8%

EMPLOYMENT LEVEL	
BLUE COLLAR	48%
WHITE COLLAR	26%
EXECUTIVE/MANAGERIAL LEVELS	26%

About the Author

This book is the twelfth that Mel Poretz has either coauthored or written on his own, the third in a series of books based on polls of what Americans are thinking. He originated and cowrote the progenitor of the series, *The First Really Important Survey of American Habits*, and wrote, also with Barry Sinrod, *Do You Do It with the Lights On?* He is the originator and a coauthor of a series of humor books entitled *Sam, The Ceiling Needs Painting*, which was published worldwide. Mel also wrote the lyrics for a children's educational album and several singles, and the lyrics for a series of children's motion pictures. A TV game show he codeveloped is currently being repackaged for European cable television production. Mel spent forty-five years in the sales promotion and marketing fields, culminating with eighteen years as owner of an East Coast fulfillment house before his retirement in 1992. He is now an Adjunct Instructor of Marketing in the Adelphi University Schools of Business, Garden City, NY.